Did You Write to Grandma?

By Jean Elsie Cox and J. Lyn Fara
Illustrated by Cecily Lang

Vocabulary Words

1. wrap
2. wreath
3. wrench
4. Wright
5. Wrinkles
6. wrist watch
   wristwatch
7. write
8. writing
9. written
10. wrong
11. wrote

Story Words

12. door
13. flowers
14. Grandma
15. Grandma's
16. hang
17. height
18. mall
19. send
20. sister's
21. squeak

Phonetic Storybook 16

Oleson Elementary
Title III LEN 04-05

Silent w, k, l, b, g, h, t •
qu = k

Raceway Steps 31–33

MODERN CURRICULUM PRESS
Pearson Learning Group

Contents

2

"Seth, have you written to Grandma yet?" asked Dad. "Her birthday is on Thursday."

"Not yet, Dad," said
Seth, "but I will write to
her right now."

"Great!" said Dad. "If
you need help writing, let
me know. We can send
your letter with Grandma's
birthday gift."

Dad began to wrap the
gift. It was a wreath made
from dried flowers to
hang on a wall or door.

Seth sat down. He
thought about what to
write.

"I could tell her about the new toys we got for Wrinkles," thought Seth. "Wrinkles likes to play with the squeak toy the best."

"Maybe I could tell her
that I got a wristwatch
like Dad's," thought Seth.

"Dad," asked Seth, "do you think Grandma might want to know about my bike? I grew so much the seat was the wrong height. You used a wrench to fix it."

"She might like to hear about your bike. She might like to hear about your new wristwatch, too," said Dad.

"Yes, Dad," said Seth, "I was going to tell her that it's just like your wristwatch."

"You could tell her who was at the mall giving away whole boxes of books today. It was Mr. Wright, your sister's teacher," said Dad.

"You're right," said Seth. "I could tell her about that, too. There's a lot to write about. I bet Grandma will be glad that I wrote to her."

"Grandma will love your letter," said Dad. "It will be the best gift that she gets for her birthday!"
The End

The Button on the Doorknob

By J. Lyn Fara

Illustrated by Dominic Catalano

Vocabulary Words

1. doorknob
   knap sack
2. knapsack
3. knees
4. knelt
5. knew
6. knife
7. knit
8. knitted
9. knob
   knock
10. knocked
11. knot
12. knowledge
13. known

14. knuckles

Story Words

15. brings
    but ton
16. button
17. climb
18. crumbs
19. either
20. floor
21. holding
    Knots ville
22. Knotsville
23. night
24. Spider
25. though

There is an old barn
in a small town called
Knotsville. Lots of animals
live in the barn. Some of
the animals only come out
at night.

18

Nan is well known to
the animals in the barn.
She comes every day to
feed and milk each cow.
She brings her lunch in
a knapsack. When she is
finished with lunch, she
hangs the knapsack on
the doorknob.

One day the knapsack had a loose button. Nan did not know the button was loose. As Nan took the knapsack off the knob, the button fell off. Mel and Max Mouse saw it fall.

Nan took a step. She knocked the button across the floor. It fell into a crack.

Nan knelt down. She tried to reach the button. The crack was too tight. Her knuckles did not fit.

Nan pulled out a plastic knife from her knapsack. She had used the knife to cut an apple for lunch. She put the knife in the crack. She tried to push out the button, but the button would not budge!

Nan got off her knees. "I guess it's stuck," she said. With that, she gave up and went home.

Nan thought she knew all the animals in the barn, but she did not know Mel and Max. They know her, though. Each night, Mel and Max enjoy the crumbs left from Nan's lunch.

Mel and Max wanted to help Nan, but they could not get the button either. They went to Miss Owl. She was known in the barn for her great knowledge.

"Please share your knowledge with us," said Mel.

"We want to help Nan get her button," said Max. "The crack is too small to climb in. It is too deep to reach in. How can we get the button?"

"You must see my friend, Sally Spider," said Miss Owl. "She can knit you a strong thread from her web. The thread can be tied to the button to pull it out of the crack."

So, Mel and Max went to see Sally Spider. Sally said she would help them. She knitted a strong thread.

Then, Sally went into the crack. She tied the thread to the button and made a knot. Sally came out of the crack holding the thread.

Mel and Max helped pull the thread and the button out of the crack. Sally went up the door. She hung the thread on the knob.

Mel and Max said, "Thanks!" to Sally.

The next morning, Nan saw her button on the knob. She was happy. To this day, Nan does not know how it got there!

The End

Pam and Her Folks

By Lynda MacDonald

Illustrated by Jane McCreary

Vocabulary Words

1. calf
2. calm
3. folks
4. half
5. palm
6. salmon
7. salve
8. should
9. stalk
10. talk
11. talking
12. walk
13. walked

Story Words

14. camped
15. butterfly
16. caterpillar
17. country
18. felt
19. itch
20. ivy
21. lake
22. leaflets
23. moose
24. peaceful
25. poison
26. tickled

Pam went with her folks. They drove in the car for half the day. They drove to the country.

They camped near a
big lake.
"This is a calm and
peaceful place," said Dad.

Pam and her folks went for a walk.

Pam saw a green
caterpillar on a stalk.

It walked on Pam's palm.
It tickled!

"Soon, it will be a
butterfly," said Pam. "It
should be free. I will let
it go."

"That's good," said her
folks.

Pam walked by a plant with three leaves on its stems. Soon, Pam felt an itch. The itch was on the calf of Pam's leg.

Mom put salve on it.
The salve helped the itch.

Mom said, "That was
poison ivy, Pam. Poison ivy
has three leaves. 'Leaflets
three, let them be.'"

"I will watch out for it,"
said Pam.

The lake was calm. So,
Dad and Pam went fishing.

"Sh," said Dad to Pam.
"Talking could scare the
fish away!"

"Sh," said Pam to the
moose calf. "Don't talk!"

Pam should get a fish with this bait. Pam fished and fished.

She waited and waited. Would Pam get a fish? Could Pam get a fish?

Yes, she did!
Wow! Maybe it's a
salmon!
The End

Gary Goldfinch's Numb Toes

By Lynda MacDonald
Illustrated by Eldon Doty

Step 32 • Silent **b**

Vocabulary Words

1. comb
2. crumb
3. debt
4. doubt
   doubted
5. lamb
6. limb
7. numb
8. plumber

Story Words

9. anymore
10. bruised
11. doesn't
12. finally
13. friend
14. Goldfinch
15. Goldfinch's
16. liftoff
17. maybe
18. screech
19. south
20. sunshine
21. toes
22. weather
    weathered

Gary Goldfinch sat on his limb. The air was getting cold. Gary was getting cold.

Gary spied a crumb on
the ground. Yum!

"My toes are getting numb. I don't like the cold and I don't like snow. It is time to go south," said Gary.

Gary packed his bag.
He put in his comb and
his last few crumbs.

"Good-bye, good-bye,
cold weather! Sunshine,
here I come!" he called.

Just as the first snow
began to fall, Gary
Goldfinch made his liftoff!
Gary flew and flew, and
the cold wind blew!

Suddenly, a big gust of wind smacked Gary! It hit him hard, and he fell to the ground.

52

Poor Gary! He bruised his wing. He could not fly. He doubted that he could go south.

Poor Gary! He hopped along the road. His wing hurt. He was cold. He was numb. His crumbs were all gone.

The road stretched on
and on. Then, up ahead,
Gary saw a lamb. Maybe
the lamb could help him.

"Would you give me a ride south, where it doesn't snow?" Gary asked the lamb.

"I'm sorry," said the lamb. "I can't take you there."

"I have a friend who is a plumber, though," the lamb said. "Maybe you could get a ride when Ray drives by here."

"Every day at two
o'clock Ray comes by this
spot on the road. Watch
for his truck, then wave.
He might stop."

That is just what Gary did! When he saw the truck, he waved his good wing in the air. He waved and waved it. Finally, the driver saw him and stopped. Screech!

"Climb in," said Ray.
"I'm a plumber, you see.
I'll make you a limb to
perch on. You can ride
here with me."

"Thank you, thank you," sang Gary. "I'm glad that we met. I'll sing you sweet songs to pay off my debt."

Gary Goldfinch came south. His toes were not numb anymore. They were warm. His wing did not hurt anymore.

Gary Goldfinch had weathered the storm!

The End

Great Gnus!

By Margaret Arvay

Illustrated by Maryann Kovalski

Vocabulary Words

assign
1. assigned

2. gnarl

gnat
3. gnats

4. gnaw

5. gnawing

6. gnu

7. gnus

Story Words

8. Crossing

9. Gomer

10. Grady

11. Grover

12. soft

13. swish

14. swished

15. walking

One hot day, three large gnus gnawed on plants and grass.

The hot sun shone on them. They swished their tails to keep the gnats away.

Suddenly, the three gnus heard a soft voice call.

"Come here," the voice said.

Grady Gnu looked up, but his job was to gnaw grass all day. He went back to doing just that!

The soft voice called again, "Come here." The call came from near the sign that said Gnu Crossing.

This time Grover Gnu stopped gnawing plants and walked to the sign.

Next to the sign, there was an old tree. There, in the gnarl of the tree, sat a monkey.

"I was assigned to watch the gnus," the monkey said. "I am a long way from home. I want to go home, but my legs are too tired from walking so far. Will you take me home?"

"Hop on my back," said Gomer Gnu. He had come to see the little monkey, too. With a swish of his tail, Gomer ran by the sign with the little monkey on his strong back. They ran all the way home!

The End

Listen! Her Honor, the Queen!

By Lynda MacDonald

Illustrated by James Williamson

Step 33 • Silent **h** and **t, qu = k**

Vocabulary Words

1. antique
2. bouquets
3. bristles
4. bustle
5. croquet
6. glisten
7. gristle
8. honor
9. hustle
10. John
11. listen
12. moisten
13. mosquitoes
14. often
15. Rhonda
16. rustle
17. thistle
18. Thomas
19. whistle

Story Words

20. beginning
21. brushes

22. busy

23. clover

24. coming

25. dragonfly

26. floors

27. group

28. lamps

29. orders

30. scrub

31. shiny

32. sponges

33. tiny

34. walls

35. who's

36. working

Queen Bee is blowing
her shiny new whistle!
She's calling the bees
from the clover and thistle!

"Do our hive honor.
Pay heed and listen!
Be a busy bee and
our home will glisten!"

"Get brushes with bristles
and scrub all the floors.
Moisten some sponges
and wipe walls and doors."

"Go to the garden. Get bouquets of flowers.

King John is coming in only two hours."

"Thomas, please hustle
and make us a treat.
Be sure no gristle is
left on the meat!
Rhonda, please set up
a game of croquet,
For soon after dinner,
the king likes to play."

"Listen! Mosquitoes!
Listen! Stand guard!

Don't let strange bugs
come into our yard!

Light the antique lamps
on every wall.

So all can see well and
no one will fall."

Such a hustle and
bustle is not often seen.
So many orders from
such a small queen!
What's going to happen
in this tiny yard,
That everyone here is
working so hard?

What is that rustle
outside in the grass?

Is that a small group
beginning to pass?

Who's that riding the big
dragonfly?

Wave hello to King John
as he goes by!

The End